# PRIVATE EYE

# DUMB BRITAIN

D0866086

Published in Great Britain
by Private Eye Productions Ltd,
6 Carlisle Street, London W1D 3BN

**www.private-eye.co.uk**

© 2007 Pressdram Ltd
ISBN 1 901784 47 3
Designed by Bridget Tisdall
Printed in Great Britain by
Clays Ltd, St Ives plc

# PRIVATE EYE

# DUMB BRITAIN

Compiled by
MARCUS BERKMANN

Illustrated by Grizelda

**Real contestants, real quiz shows,
real answers, real dumb!**

# THE SYLLABUS

# ART

ANNE ROBINSON: If a woman is known as Rubenesque, meaning she has a voluptuous figure, which 17th-century artist is she named after?

CONTESTANT: Aretha Franklin.

*The Weakest Link*

PRESENTER: Name a film starring Bob Hoskins that is also the name of a famous painting by Leonardo da Vinci.

CONTESTANT: Who Framed Roger Rabbit.

*Rock FM, Preston*

JIM BOWEN: Which artist is famous for his drawings of fat little girls on fat little ponies?

CONTESTANT: Is it Turner, Jim?

*Bullseye, Challenge*

ANNE ROBINSON: Who painted The Laughing Cavalier? Franz...?

CONTESTANT: Liszt.

*The Weakest Link*

PRESENTER: Was Paul Cezanne an impressionist or a ventriloquist?

CONTESTANT: Ventriloquist.

*Deadly Knowledge Show, C4*

EAMONN HOLMES: In Leonardo da Vinci's painting The Last Supper, how many people are depicted?

CONTESTANT: 40.

*National Lottery Jet Set*

ANNE ROBINSON: Where is the Mona Lisa
  hung?
CONTESTANT: The British Museum.

*The Weakest Link*

MATT WOODLEY: Name the artist born
  in 1776 in East Bergholt, Suffolk, whose
  paintings include The Hay Wain and The
  Chain Pier, Brighton.
CONTESTANT: Van Gogh.

*BBC Radio Devon*

RICHARD BACON: Which artist had a blue
  period?
CONTESTANT: Stalin.

*XFM*

# BIOLOGY &
# NATURAL HISTORY

ANNE ROBINSON: What black-and-white
  bird should you salute if you see it on its
  own?
CONTESTANT: A penguin.

*The Weakest Link*

DALE WINTON: Which bird lays its eggs in other birds' nests? Is it (a) jackdaw, (b) cuckoo, or (c) magpie?

CONTESTANT: Well, it's not a cuckoo because that lives in a clock.

*National Lottery: In It To Win It*


ANNE ROBINSON: In nature, the teal and the mallard are species of which water bird?

CONTESTANT: Eagle.

*The Weakest Link*


STEVE WRIGHT: What is the north American word for elk?

CONTESTANT: Pine.

*Radio 2*


EAMONN HOLMES: Which tree produces the acorn?

CONTESTANT: The acorn tree.

*National Lottery Jet Set*


NICK KNOWLES: Which disease killed thousands of British trees in 1970s and 1980s?

CONTESTANT: Myxomatosis.

*Judgemental, BBC1*

STEVE WRIGHT: A sapling is a young what?

CONTESTANT: Pig.

*Radio 2*

ANNE ROBINSON: Which animal builds dams and ledges?

CONTESTANT: Sheep.

*The Weakest Link*

STEVE WRIGHT: What is a female sheep called?

CONTESTANT: Er... er... a goat.

*Radio 2*

PRESENTER: What black-and-white animal are some police vehicles named after?

CONTESTANT: Zebras.

*Kiss FM*

GARY KING: What British mammal lives in a sett and has a distinctive black-and-white striped head?

CONTESTANT: A zebra.

*LBC 97.3*

PRESENTER: How long is it since dinosaurs roamed the earth?

CONTESTANT: 800 years.

*Heart FM*

LES DENNIS: Name an animal that makes people scream.

CONTESTANT: A squirrel.

*Family Fortunes, Challenge*

HOST: We're looking for 'Films with an Animal in the Title' – like Spiderman or Catwoman.

CALLER: Lassie.

HOST: Sorry, no, that was the animal's name, it's not actually a title that includes the name of an animal, is it? Next caller.

2ND CALLER: Free Willy.

HOST: No, sorry, you've done the same thing. We want a film with the name of an animal in it, not a film that's an animal's name. Next caller...

3RD CALLER: Bambi.

HOST: No, that's not the name of the animal, it's the animal's name. Do you see? Because in that film, Bambi was the name of the dog.

*Big Game Quiz, ftn*

GARY KING: What is the only mammal that sleeps on its back?

DARREN from Bexleyheath: Er... a whale?

*LBC 97.3*

CHAPPERS (or possibly Dave): What do you call the fat on a whale?

CONTESTANT: Chewing gum.

*Chappers & Dave show, Radio 1*

ANNE ROBINSON: 'Bolster' is an anagram of which marine crustacean?

CONTESTANT: Crab.

*The Weakest Link*

CHRIS MOYLES: Which 'S' is a kind of whale that can grow up to 80 tonnes?

CONTESTANT: Um...

MOYLES: It begins with 'S' and rhymes with 'perm'.

CONTESTANT: Shark.

*Radio 1*

# CAREERS ADVICE

GREG SCOTT: We're looking for an occupation beginning with 'T'.

CONTESTANT: Doctor.

SCOTT: No, it's 'T'. 'T' for Tommy. 'T' for Tango. 'T' for Tintinnabulation.

CONTESTANT: Oh right... (pause)... Doctor.

*Quizmania, ITV1*

CHUCK THOMAS: OK, caller, can you give me an occupation beginning with 'S'?

CONTESTANT: Er... psychiatrist?

*Quizmania*

STEVE WRIGHT: What does a fletcher make?

CONTESTANT: Curtains.

*Radio 2*

CHUCK THOMAS: He works in a circus, makes children laugh, looks like Ronald McDonald and rhymes with 'frown'. For a possible £4,000, what is he?

CONTESTANT: A joker.

*Quizmania*

STEVE WRIGHT: People in which profession are often described as 'the gnomes of Zurich'?

CONTESTANT: Opticians.

*Radio 2*

GARY KING: Name the funny men who once entertained kings and queens at court.

CONTESTANT: Lepers.

*LBC 97.3*

# CLASSICS &
# ANCIENT HISTORY

STEVE WRIGHT: Which month of the year is named after the Roman god of war?

CONTESTANT: Thursday.

*Radio 2*


ANNE ROBINSON: Which Roman statesman gave his name to the month of July?

CONTESTANT: Augustus.

*The Weakest Link*


ANNE ROBINSON: What word for an ancient Roman marketplace is also a site on the internet for open discussion?

CONTESTANT: Chatroom.

*The Weakest Link*


RICHARD ALLINSON: What international brand shares its name with the Greek goddess of victory?

CONTESTANT (after long deliberation): Erm, Kelloggs?

*Radio 2*

ANNE ROBINSON: In dinosaurs, what does the T stand for in 'T Rex'?

CONTESTANT: Thesaurus.

*The Weakest Link*

ANNE ROBINSON: When the twins Romulus and Remus were abandoned in Rome, they were suckled by which four-legged creature?

CONTESTANT: The minotaur.

*The Weakest Link*

STEVE WRIGHT: The mythical minotaur had the body of a man and the head of a what?

CONTESTANT: Millipede.

*Radio 2*

ANNE ROBINSON: What G was the complex knot severed by Alexander the Great in the fourth century BC?

CONTESTANT: Granny.

*The Weakest Link*

ANNE ROBINSON: Which warrior queen, who fought against the Romans, is sometimes said to be buried under a platform in King's Cross Station?

CONTESTANT: Joan of Arc.

*The Weakest Link*

ANNE ROBINSON: Watling Street, which now forms part of the A5, was built by which ancient civilisation?

CONTESTANT: Apes.

*The Weakest Link*

# DOMESTIC SCIENCE

ANNE ROBINSON: What sweet substance made by insects is eaten with yogurt in Greece?

UNIDENTIFIED POP STAR: Houmous.

*The Weakest Link*

JOHN HUMPHRYS: Which breakfast cereal is also slang for a period of imprisonment?

CONTESTANT: Cheerios.

*Mastermind, BBC2*

GARY KING: What was the first name of Mr Birdseye, the inventor of Frozen food?

CONTESTANT: Captain.

*LBC 97.3*

## DUMB WORLD

PRESENTER: Please conclude the following nursery rhyme: 'Little Miss Muffet sat on a tuffet, eating her... ' what?

A: Roti prata.
B: Curds and whey.
C: Beef rendang.
D: Chicken rice.

CONTESTANT: A: Roti prata.

*Who Wants To Be A Millionaire?*
*SINGAPORE*

ANNE ROBINSON: What is a two-word phrase describing tinned haricots in tomato sauce?

CONTESTANT: Egg mayonnaise.

*The Weakest Link*

MELANIE SYKES: You are eating a baklava. Are you having a main course or a pudding?

CONTESTANT: A starter.

*Today With Des And Mel, ITV*

BOB HOLNESS: What 'L' is the meat that goes into shepherd's pie?

CONTESTANT: Luncheon.

*Blockbusters, Challenge*

PRESENTER: Cambridge, Atkins and Cabbage Soup are all types of what?

CONTESTANT: Universities?

*Radio Clyde*

ANNE ROBINSON: The cultivation of which fruit is known as viniculture?

CONTESTANT: Potatoes.

*The Weakest Link*

ANNE ROBINSON: In America it's known as Jello. Which letter is changed to give the British equivalent?

CONTESTANT: W.

*The Weakest Link*

PRESENTER: Which English queen is the cocktail 'Bloody Mary' named after?

CONTESTANT: Is it Margherita?

*BBC GMR*

GARY KING: What's the main ingredient of a Molotov cocktail?

CONTESTANT: Vodka?

*LBC 97.3*

LES DENNIS: Name something you do after a long walk.

CONTESTANT: Rub black pudding onto your feet.

*Family Fortunes, Challenge*


LES DENNIS: Name a TV chef.

CONTESTANT: Rolf Harris.

SECOND CONTESTANT: Mrs Beeton.

THIRD CONTESTANT: My mum.

*Family Fortunes, Challenge*


ANNE ROBINSON: Which celebrity chef, whose first name begins with an 'H', has the surname 'Fearnley-Whittingstall'?

CONTESTANT: Rick Stein.

*The Weakest Link*


# ECONOMICS


STEVE WRIGHT: Which British decimal coin ceased production in 1983?

CONTESTANT: 50p.

*Radio 2*

# ENGINEERING

CONTESTANT: You step in it and it takes you up and down to different floors.

RICHARD MADELEY: Dog poo?

*'You Say We Pay', Richard And Judy, Channel 4*

# ENGLISH LANGUAGE

BOB HOLNESS: What 'E' was invented by Ludwic Lazarus Zamenhof in 1887 in the hope that it would become the world's universal language?

CONTESTANT: English.

*Blockbusters, Challenge*

ANNE ROBINSON: Which word links an operation on the heart with a detour around a town or a village?

CONTESTANT: Ring road.

*The Weakest Link*

DALE WINTON: What type of weapon was a claymore? Was it (a) a mace, (b) a sword, or (c) a dagger?

CONTESTANT: Well I know it can't be mace, as the police have only just started using that.

*National Lottery: In It To Win It*

ANNE ROBINSON: Complete this three-word phrase meaning 'haphazard': 'hit and...'

CONTESTANT: Run.

*The Weakest Link*


ANNE ROBINSON: The term 'gyppy' that describes a stomach upset is derived from the name of which African country?

CONTESTANT: Venezuela.

*The Weakest Link*


GREG SCOTT: We're looking for a word that goes in front of 'clock'.

CONTESTANT: 'Grandfather'.

GREG SCOTT: 'Grandfather clock' is already up there. Say something else.

CONTESTANT: 'Panda'.

*Quizmania*


ANNE ROBINSON: What name rhyming with 'tapper' was given to girls in the 1920s who wore fringed dresses and danced the Charleston?

CONTESTANT: Slapper.

*The Weakest Link*

GEORGE JONES: What are secateurs used for?

CONTESTANT: They work in offices.

*Radio Ulster*

SARA COX: Complete this well-known saying: 'Beauty is in the eye of the...'

CONTESTANT: Tiger.

*Radio 1*

ANNE ROBINSON: Which 'D' normally refers to the male parent?

CONTESTANT: Mum.

*The Weakest Link*

ANNE ROBINSON: What 'Z' is used to describe a human who has returned from the dead?

CONTESTANT: Unicorn.

*The Weakest Link*


ANNE ROBINSON: What 'T' is a term for both an item of underwear and also a rising column of warm air?

CONTESTANT: Turtle.

*The Weakest Link*


ANNE ROBINSON: In clubs and societies, which word for a dark-coloured spherical object means to veto?

CONTESTANT: Pardon?

ROBINSON: (steelier) In clubs and societies, which word for a dark-coloured spherical object means to veto?

CONTESTANT: Custard.

*The Weakest Link*


EAMONN HOLMES: What is the sincerest form of flattery?

CONTESTANT: Sarcasm.

*National Lottery Jet-Set*

STEVE WRIGHT: On which mode of transport would you find a crow's nest?

CONTESTANT: A plane.

*Radio 2*

ANNE ROBINSON: In human development, what 'B' is the usual four-letter word for a newborn infant?

LIZ BREWER: Sorry, could you repeat the question?

ROBINSON: In human development, what 'b' is the usual four-letter word for a newborn infant?

LIZ BREWER: Wasp.

*The Weakest Link*

ANNE ROBINSON: Which illness is named after its high temperature and red skin colouration?

CONTESTANT: Yellow fever.

*The Weakest Link*


DALE WINTON: On a ship, what is a blue peter? Is it (a) a crow's nest, (b) a flag, or (c) an anchor?

CONTESTANT: Well, I remember from watching Blue Peter, that they used to give out badges shaped like an anchor.

*National Lottery: In It To Win It*


EAMONN HOLMES: Name the famous Scotsman who gave his name to a type of raincoat.

CONTESTANT: Is it Duffel, Eamonn?

*National Lottery Jet Set*


RICHARD ALLINSON: What is the name of the powdered tobacco that is sniffed through the nose?

CONTESTANT: Cocaine.

*Radio 2*

ANNE ROBINSON: The name of which small wingless jumping insect precedes 'bite', 'collar' and 'market' to give three familiar terms?

CONTESTANT: Bicycle.

*The Weakest Link*

LES DENNIS: Apart from a guernsey, name an item of clothing named after a place.

CONTESTANT: Kilt.

SECOND CONTESTANT: Beret.

THIRD CONTESTANT: Sandals.

FOURTH CONTESTANT: Sari.

*Family Fortunes, Challenge*

EAMONN HOLMES: Which European airline's name is made up of three consecutive letters from the alphabet?

CONTESTANT: (blank stare)

HOLMES: You know. From the alphabet. Three letters in a row.

CONTESTANT: Aer Lingus.

*National Lottery Jet Set*


LES DENNIS: Give another word for telltale.

CONTESTANT: Telltale.

*Family Fortunes, Challenge*


LES DENNIS: Name another way to say 'be quiet'.

CONTESTANT: Magpie.

SECOND CONTESTANT: Be quiet.

*Family Fortunes, Challenge*


PHIL WOOD: What's another name for the 'green eyed monster'?

CONTESTANT: The sugar plum fairy.

*BBC GMR*

# ENGLISH LITERATURE

DAVE BUSSEY: Name the Danish man who wrote such fairy tales as Thumbelina and The Ugly Duckling.

CONTESTANT (after long pause): Would it be Enid Blyton?

*Radio Lincolnshire*


ANNE ROBINSON: Finish this well known rhyme: 'Ding dong bell, pussy's in the...'

CONTESTANT: Kitchen.

*The Weakest Link*


DALE WINTON: In Shakespeare's play A Midsummer Night's Dream, who was king of the fairies?

CONTESTANT: I'm not very good at history.

*National Lottery: In It To Win It*


JOHN HUMPHRYS: Which character in Hamlet speaks the words 'neither a borrower or lender be'?

CONTESTANT: Yorick.

*Mastermind, BBC2*

GARY KING: Who was Mary Arden's famous son?

CONTESTANT: Can I have a clue?

KING: Yes. He was famous around the Globe!

CONTESTANT: Bill Gates?

*LBC 97.3*

GORDON BURNS: In Shakespeare, which character says, 'Friends, Romans, countrymen, lend me your ears'?

CONTESTANT: Richard III

*The Krypton Factor, ftn*

ANNE ROBINSON: What word means the opposite of dystopia and was also the title of a book by Thomas More?

CONTESTANT: Myopia.

*The Weakest Link*


ANNE ROBINSON: Which author of The Decline And Fall Of The Roman Empire shares his name with a long-armed ape?

CONTESTANT: Gorilla.

*The Weakest Link*


ANNE ROBINSON: In Alexander Pope's poem, what 'springs eternal in the human breast'?

CONTESTANT: Milk.

*The Weakest Link*


GARY KING: Which author wrote Bleak House?

CONTESTANT: Jane Eyre.

*LBC 97.3*


STEVE WRIGHT: Who wrote the controversial novel Lady Chatterley's Lover?

CONTESTANT: Chaucer.

*Radio 2*

SARA COX: What was Bram Stoker's most famous creation?

CONTESTANT: Was it Branston Pickle, Sara?

*Radio 1*

ANNE ROBINSON: What is name of the building Charles Dickens once lived in and which gave its name to one of his most famous novels?

CONTESTANT: Er... Great Expectations?

*The Weakest Link, BBC2*

CRAIG STEVENS: We're looking for a four-letter answer here – Shakespeare said that this by any other name would smell as sweet...

CONTESTANT: Soap?

*Brainteaser, Five*

ANNE ROBINSON: The cult novel The Naked Lunch was written by William... what?

CONTESTANT: Wordsworth.

*The Weakest Link*

## DUMB WORLD

JAMES O'LOGHLIN: Which of Shakespeare's plays is set in the Italian city of Verona?

CONTESTANT: The Merchant Of Venice.

*ABC Radio 702, Sydney, AUSTRALIA*

DALE WINTON: Boo Radley is a character in which prize-winning 1960s novel?

TWO CONTESTANTS: (after conferring) Pride And Prejudice.

*The National Lottery: In It To Win It*

ROBERT ROBINSON: The author of the influential 1963 book The Feminine Mystique and co-founder of the National Organization of Women in the USA died this year at the age of 85. What was her name?

CONTESTANT: Bette Midler.

*Brain of Britain, Radio 4*

ANNE ROBINSON: Which novel by Joseph Heller starts with the words 'It was love at first sight...'?

CONTESTANT: Anna Karenina.

*The Weakest Link*

ANNE ROBINSON: Which animals feature in the book Watership Down?

CONTESTANT: Was it beavers, Anne?

*The Weakest Link*

JAMES O'BRIEN: Who wrote Charlie and the Chocolate Factory?

CONTESTANT: T S Eliot.

*LBC 97.3*


JIM BOWEN: Which aristocratic character was created by Frances Hodgson Burnett?

CONTESTANT: Count Dracula.

*Bullseye, Challenge*


ANNE ROBINSON: What 'T' is a novel by Irvine Welsh featuring the characters Begbie, Renton and Sick Boy?

CONTESTANT: Treasure Island.

*The Weakest Link*


EAMONN HOLMES: Who wrote Treasure Island?

CONTESTANT: Robinson Crusoe.

*National Lottery Jet Set*


STEVE YABSLEY: Which book by Graham Greene was set in Brighton?

CONTESTANT: Fawlty Towers?

*BBC Radio Bristol*

# GAMES

LES DENNIS: Name a game you can play in the bath.

CONTESTANT: Scuba diving.

*Family Fortunes, Challenge*

EAMONN HOLMES: Which snooker player's nickname was 'the Whirlwind'?

CONTESTANT: Hurricane Higgins.

*Sudo-Q, BBC2*

ANNE ROBINSON: Which Ossie played for
'Tottingham' in the FA Cup Final?
CONTESTANT: Ossie Osbourne.

*The Weakest Link*

SARA COX: Who was the first black manager
of an English Premier League side?
CONTESTANT: Ron Atkinson.

*Radio 1*

NEMONE: Who was the first black footballer to captain England?

CONTESTANT: Alan Shearer.

*6Music*

NEIL FOX: Which team won in the 2005 Euro Women's football final?

CONTESTANT: Australia.

NEIL FOX: How do you know?

CONTESTANT: Because I watched it on television.

NEIL FOX: Well, it was Germany.

*The Big Call, Scottish TV*

JOHN HUMPHRYS: Which stretch of water did comedian David Walliams swim across in 10 hours 34 minutes?

CONTESTANT: The Atlantic.

*Weakest Link*

ALAN BRAZIL: So, to win the tickets for the match, can you tell me the distance in miles between Chelsea's ground Stamford Bridge and the Olympic Stadium in Athens?

CONTESTANT: Is it 50,000 miles, Alan?

*talkSPORT*

# DUMB WORLD

JOHN: I'm not sure about this question, given that your name is Philip Hill. But anyway. Who was the only American-born driver to have won the Formula One world championship? Was it Phil Hill, or Mika Häkkinen?

CONTESTANT (actually called Philip Hill): Umm, could I have the names again?

JOHN: Yes. Was it (puts on strong American accent) Phil Hill, or was it (pronounces it as though it's a weird foreign name) Mika Häkkinen?

CONTESTANT: Er, Mika Häkkinen?

Ross: Aaargh! No. OK, contestant number 2, who do you reckon it was?

Contestant 2: Er, the American guy. Mike something?

Ross: Phil Hill? That's right!

*The Breakfast Show with Ross and John,*
*3 AW Melbourne, AUSTRALIA*

DOM (or possibly Dick): In which city were the recent Winter Olympics held?

CONTESTANT: Taunton.

*Dick & Dom In Da Bungalow, BBC1*

DANNY KELLY: Which country do the rugby team the All Blacks represent?

CONTESTANT: Is it Africa?

KELLY: No, no, keep going...

CONTESTANT: Jamaica?

*BBC WM*

PRESENTER: How many pins do you need to knock over for a strike in 10-pin bowling?

CONTESTANT: WELL, ALL OF THEM.

PRESENTER: And that's how many?

CONTESTANT: 9.

*BBC Radio Leicester*

PRESENTER: OK, let me rephrase that. Against which country did England draw 0-0 in yesterday's England v Macedonia game?

CALLER: No, sorry, I still don't know.

*Virgin Radio*

MICHAEL BARRYMORE: What did Roger
Bannister do in under four minutes in
1954?

CONTESTANT: Orbit the earth?

*Strike It Rich, Challenge*

# GEOGRAPHY

ANNE ROBINSON: The M27 links
Southampton with which other south coast
city?

CONTESTANT: Leeds.

*The Weakest Link*

JAMIE THEAKSTON: In which English county is the peninsula known as 'the Lizard'?

CONTESTANT: Shropshire.

*Beg, Borrow or Steal, BBC2*

LES DENNIS: Name someone associated with Liverpool.

CONTESTANT: My uncle Peter.

*Family Fortunes, Challenge*

GRAEME GARDEN: What is the highest mountain in England?

CONTESTANT (after long pause): Everest.

*Beat The Nation, C4*

ANNE ROBINSON: What is the highest mountain in Scotland, Ben... what?

CONTESTANT: Ben Everest.

*The Weakest Link*

EAMONN HOLMES: Ben Nevis is situated in which mountain range?

CONTESTANT: The Himalayas.

*National Lottery Jet-Set*

DALE WINTON: Skegness is a seaside resort on the coast of which sea: (a) Irish Sea, (b) English Channel, (c) North Sea?

CONTESTANT: Oh I know that, you can start writing out the cheque now Dale. It's on the east coast, so it must be the Irish Sea.

*National Lottery: In It To Win It*

EAMONN HOLMES: Where are the Brecon Beacons?

CONTESTANT: Salisbury Plain.

*National Lottery Jet-Set*

ANNE ROBINSON: The Solway Firth lies in between England and which other UK country?

CONTESTANT: Spain.

*The Weakest Link*


STEVE WRIGHT: In which county would you be if you visited Great Yarmouth, Fakenham and Norwich?

CONTESTANT: East Anglia.

WRIGHT: No, that's the region. In which county would you be?

CONTESTANT: Er... Devon?

*Radio 2*


ANNE ROBINSON: The Suez Canal links the Red Sea with which other body of water?

CONTESTANT: The Thames?

*The Weakest Link*


ANNE ROBINSON: Into what body of water does the River Thames flow?

CONTESTANT (after long pause): The Atlantic.

*The Weakest Link*

PRESENTER: What is the capital of Ethiopia?
CONTESTANT: Bangladesh.

*Radio Galaxy, Sheffield*

EAMONN HOLMES: What is the capital of
Belgium?
CONTESTANT: Luxembourg.

*National Lottery Jet Set*

## DUMB WORLD

PRESENTER: Name
the capital of Iraq.
CONTESTANT: Can
you spell that please?
PRESENTER: I-R-A-Q.
CONTESTANT: What was the
question again?
PRESENTER: Name the capital of
Iraq.
CONTESTANT: I'm going to go
with Afghanistan.

*Beauty and the Geek,*
*WBDC, Washington DC, AMERICA*

ANNE ROBINSON: Bratislava is the capital of which eastern European nation?

CONTESTANT: Er, Alaska?

*The Weakest Link*

STEVE WRIGHT: What is the capital of Switzerland? Be careful with this one.

CONTESTANT: Munich.

*Radio 2*

GABBY LOGAN: Which Scottish town is known as the Granite City?

CONTESTANT: Stockholm.

*The Vault, ITV*

STEVE WRIGHT: Which European capital city is known as the Eternal City?

CONTESTANT: Erm, New York, Steve?

*Radio 2*

ANNE ROBINSON: What is the capital of Saudi Arabia?

CONTESTANT (and eventual winner): Tel Aviv.

*The Weakest Link*

STEVE WRIGHT: In which European city would you find Las Ramblas and Park Güell?

CONTESTANT: (agonised silence)

WRIGHT: I'll give you a clue. It's a Spanish city.

CONTESTANT: Rome.

*Radio 2*


ANNE ROBINSON: The cedar tree appears on the flag of which Middle Eastern country with a coastline on the Mediterranean?

CONTESTANT: Canada.

*The Weakest Link*


ANNE ROBINSON: Which middle-east country's flag consists of a quotation from the Koran in white on a green background?

CONTESTANT: Israel.

*The Weakest Link*


LES DENNIS: Name something associated with Egypt.

CONTESTANT: Cigars.

*Family Fortunes, Challenge*

PRESENTER: In which country would you find Miami?

CONTESTANT: Uh... pass.

PRESENTER: In which city would you find the Eiffel Tower?

SAME CONTESTANT London.

*Star 107 FM, Cambridgeshire*

ANNE ROBINSON: Which group of islands, famous for its distinctive knitwear, is off the west coast of Ireland?

CONTESTANT: The Galapagos Islands.

*The Weakest Link*

ANNE ROBINSON: Which European country does Gibraltar have a border with?

CONTESTANT: Greece.

*The Weakest Link*

DALE WINTON: In which country are the ruins of the ancient city of Troy? Is it (a) Tunisia, (b) Italy or (c) Turkey?

CONTESTANT: I think this is when all those years doing A-level Ancient History will start to pay off. (pause) Well it's not Turkey.

*National Lottery: In It To Win It*

PRESENTER: Which country did the Panama hat originate from?

CONTESTANT: Luton.

*BBC Radio Norfolk*

ANNE ROBINSON: Which European country shares its name with a type of bird?

CONTESTANT: Greece.

*The Weakest Link*

ANNE ROBINSON: Which 'D' is an area of Holland famous for its distinctive pottery?

CONTESTANT: Denmark.

*The Weakest Link*

ANNE ROBINSON: Which Lebanese airport has the IATA code 'BEY'?

CONTESTANT: Beijing.

*The Weakest Link*

SIMON BATES: What was the name of the hurricane that devastated the city of New Orleans in August 2005?

CONTESTANT: (very long pause) Hm, I'm going to have to guess. Freddy?

*Classic FM*

ANNE ROBINSON: Which country in South America is named after the revolutionary and explorer Simon Bolivar?

CONTESTANT: Brazil.

*The Weakest Link*

# MATHEMATICS

PRESENTER: What is 9 times 20?
CONTESTANT: 180.
PRESENTER: Well done. Good addition.

*Radio Mercury*

ANNE ROBINSON: What is the only even
number that is also a prime number?
CONTESTANT: 9.

*The Weakest Link, BBC2*

PHIL WOOD: What's 11 squared?
CONTESTANT: I don't know.
PHIL: I'll give you a clue. It's two ones with a
two in the middle.
CONTESTANT: Is it 5?

*BBC GMR*

VERNON KAY: What 'T' is left if you take 93
from 106?
ANDREA CATHERWOOD (ITN newscaster):
9.

*Vernon Kay's Gameshow Marathon, ITV2*

ANNE ROBINSON: In geometry, a solid
   object has how many dimensions?
CONTESTANT: 6.

*The Weakest Link*

ANNE ROBINSON: How many sides does an
   octohedron have?
CONTESTANT: 3.

*The Weakest Link*

STEVE WRIGHT: How many months are there
   in six years?
CONTESTANT: 46.

*Radio 2*

PRESENTER: How many toes would three
   people have in total?
CONTESTANT: 23.

*Early morning show, Radio 1*

## DUMB WORLD

PRESENTER: From what platform number did Harry Potter catch the train to Hogwarts?

CONTESTANT: Er... I don't know, and I've seen the movie.

PRESENTER: OK, what's three plus three?

CONTESTANT: Six.

PRESENTER: What's six plus three?

CONTESTANT: Nine.

PRESENTER: What's nine plus three-quarters?

CONTESTANT: Er... um... eleven?

*92 More FM, Christchurch, NEW ZEALAND*

STEVE WRIGHT: How many days are there in five weeks?

CONTESTANT: Don't know.

WRIGHT: Give it a guess.

CONTESTANT: 60.

*Radio 2*

FEARNE COTTON: How many years are there in a millennium?

CONTESTANT: 100.

COTTON: Correct.

*Radio 1*

ANNE ROBINSON: Counting down, what is the next number after 89?

CONTESTANT: 80.

*The Weakest Link*

# MEDIA STUDIES (1)

LES DENNIS: Name a character from The Wizard Of Oz.

CONTESTANT: The frog.

*Family Fortunes, Challenge*

JEREMY PAXMAN: Dubbed 'the Sphinx' in the 1920s on account of her taciturn manner off-screen, which Hollywood actress retired from public life in 1941?

OXFORD STUDENTS (after conferring): Julie Andrews.

*University Challenge, BBC2*

ANNE ROBINSON: He was known as the
King of the Cowboys. He was Roy who?

CONTESTANT: Keane.

*The Weakest Link*

STEVE WRIGHT: Who stars opposite Jude
Law in the film Cold Mountain?

CONTESTANT: Ethel Merman.

*Radio 2*

NEMONE: Can you name two members of the
comedy group the Goodies?

CONTESTANT: Peter Cook and... er...

NEMONE: No.

*6Music*

ANNE ROBINSON: Which movie star was married to Humphrey Bogart and was also a cousin of the former Prime Minister of Israel, Shimon Peres?

CONTESTANT: Gene Kelly.

*The Weakest Link*


DANNY KELLY: Which French Mediterranean town hosts a famous film festival every year?

CONTESTANT: I don't know. I need a clue.

KELLY: OK. What do beans come in?

CONTESTANT: Cartons?

*BBC Radio WM*


ANNE ROBINSON: Which animated cartoon bear has a name that suggests he's a follower of Hindu philosophy?

CONTESTANT: Paddington.

*The Weakest Link*


ANNE ROBINSON: Several characters in the Muppet Show, including Miss Piggy and Fozzie Bear, and the character Yoda in the Star Wars films were voiced by Frank who?

CONTESTANT: Carson.

*The Weakest Link*

ANNE ROBINSON: In which film did Harry Lime say, 'In Switzerland they had brotherly love and they had 500 years of democracy and peace. And what did they produce? The cuckoo clock!"?

ENGLAND CRICKETER: One Flew Over The Cuckoo Clock.

*The Weakest Link*


JIM BOWEN: Who was that person with blonde hair, on the film clip of Summer Holiday, dancing with Una Stubbs?

CONTESTANT: Sorry Jim, no idea.

BOWEN: That's all right. 'It Ain't Half Hot Mum', Melvyn...

CONTESTANT (excited): Melvyn Bragg!

*Bullseye, Challenge*


JUDI SPIERS: If a person came from Ambridge, what would be the name of the radio soap?

CONTESTANT: Er, I can't think.

SPIERS: A clue. What would you be if you used a bow and arrow?

CONTESTANT: Robin Hood.

*BBC Radio Devon*

ANNE ROBINSON: In the 2006 TV drama series Robin Hood, Keith Allen played the villain, the Sheriff of... where?

WINNER OF LADETTE TO LADY: Pass.

*The Weakest Link*

STEVE WRIGHT: Who played the title role in the 1970s show The Six Million Dollar Man?

CONTESTANT: Steve Austin.

STEVE WRIGHT: No, that was the character. We want the actor.

CONTESTANT: Majors! John Majors!

*Radio 2*

## DUMB WORLD

PRESENTER: What is the name of the long-running TV comedy show about pensioners, 'Last of the...'?

CALLER: Mohicans.

*RTE Radio 2fm, IRELAND*

ANNE ROBINSON: Which daily newspaper has the nickname 'the Grauniad' because of its large number of typographical errors?

CONTESTANT: The Mirror.

*The Weakest Link*

ANNE ROBINSON: What national newspaper is nicknamed 'the Torygraph'?

CONTESTANT: The Times.

*The Weakest Link*

JIM DAVIS (exasperated): Name any British actor.

CALLER: Mel Gibson?

*Quiz of the Week, LBC 97.3*

GRAHAM HUGHES: What is Reuters?
FEMALE CALLER: Er... can you spell that?
HUGHES: R-E-U-T-E-R-S.
MALE VOICE IN BACKGROUND: A disease!

*BBC Radio Cambridgeshire*

# MEDIA STUDIES (2)

BIG BROTHER: Who was the first English
   monarch to be divorced?
AISLEYNE: What's a monarch?
BIG BROTHER: A king or queen.
AISLEYNE: Oh... Charles.

*Big Brother, C4*

BIG BROTHER: Who was the youngest
   member of the Beatles?
AISLEYNE: Bono.

*Big Brother*

BIG BROTHER: Which bird is the fastest
   swimmer?
AISLEYNE: (silence, puzzled look) Birds don't
   swim, they fly.

*Big Brother*

BIG BROTHER: In what year did man first land on the moon?

IMOGEN: 1903.

*Big Brother*

BIG BROTHER: In Roman numerals, what does 'L' stand for?

IMOGEN: Laughing.

*Big Brother*

BIG BROTHER: In what year did the Second World War start?

SASKIA: 1966.

*Big Brother*

BIG BROTHER: How many days are there in a leap year?

IMOGEN: There are 365 days in a normal year... [much agonising]... so... 360.

*Big Brother*


GLYNN: Susie [the new 43-year-old golden ticket-winning housewife] is like Mrs Robinson.

MIKEY: Who is Mrs Robinson?

GLYNN: It's like this older woman that you have sex with, who is married.

MIKEY: Do you know her?

GLYNN: No. There's this song by Simon and Garfunkel...

MIKEY: Yeah, I know the song, yeah... but is it a song or is it an actual person?

*Big Brother*


# MEDICINE

ANNE ROBINSON: Which part of the human body consists of 33 vertebrae?

CONTESTANT: The heart.

*The Weakest Link*

LES DENNIS: Name a part of the body everyone has only one of.

CONTESTANT: Big toe.

SECOND CONTESTANT: Combine harvester.

THIRD CONTESTANT: Wedding tackle.

*Family Fortunes, Challenge*


DANNY KELLY: Where is the auditory canal?

CALLER: Is it Manchester?

*BBC Radio WM*


# MODERN HISTORY

STEVE WRIGHT: Who commanded the Norman invasion of England in 1066?

CONTESTANT: Napoleon.

*Radio 2*


ANNE ROBINSON: Which survey, completed in 1086, was used to resolve a legal dispute more than 800 years later?

CONTESTANT: The Great Fire of London.

*The Weakest Link*

EAMONN HOLMES: King Robert I of
   Scotland was popularly known by what
   other name?

CONTESTANT: Bob.

*National Lottery Jet Set*


PRESENTER: The Battle of Bosworth Field
   was the last battle in what long war?

CONTESTANT: The Boer War?

PRESENTER: I'll give you a clue. It was in
   1485.

CONTESTANT: The Crimean?

*BBC Radio Gloucestershire*


STEVE WRIGHT: Who was Commander
   of the British Fleet against the Spanish
   Armada?

CONTESTANT: Christopher Columbus.

*Radio 2*


ANNE ROBINSON: The Thirty Years War in
   Europe began in 1618 and ended in which
   year?

CONTESTANT: Oh I don't know... 1697.

*The Weakest Link*

JOHNNY VAUGHAN: When was the Great
    Fire of London?
CONTESTANT: 1962.
NEXT CONTESTANT: 1066.

*Capital Radio*

ANNE ROBINSON: Who rode out of Boston
    at midnight to warn of the redcoats' arrival:
    Paul Revere or Billy Butlin?
CONTESTANT: Billy Butlin.

*The Weakest Link*

ANNE ROBINSON: In history, Emma Hamilton was the mistress of which English admiral?

CONTESTANT: Napoleon.

*The Weakest Link*

PRESENTER: Who said 'Kiss me Hardy'?

CONTESTANT: Was it his girlfriend?

PRESENTER: No, it was a man who said it.

CONTESTANT: Was it Stan Laurel?

*Magic 1152, Manchester*

ANNE ROBINSON: Which English Duke commanded the army that defeated Napoleon at the battle of Waterloo?

CONTESTANT: Edinburgh.

*The Weakest Link*

DJ DANNY: Napoleon died in St Helen's (sic) on this day 165 years ago. What did he say on his death bed?

LISA from Doncaster: 'Kiss me, Hardy.'

(Fanfare.)

DJ DANNY: You're right!

*Magic AM, South Yorks*

ANNE ROBINSON: Which ship started its round-the-world voyage in 1831 with Charles Darwin as its on-board naturalist?

CONTESTANT: The Marie Rose Celeste.

*The Weakest Link*

PRESENTER: Prince Albert was married to which Queen?

CONTESTANT (after some thought): Er... Natalie?

*Christmas Day quiz, TalkSPORT*

ANNE ROBINSON: In catering, a famous chain of tea shops and so-called 'corner houses' was opened in London in 1894 by Joseph who?

CONTESTANT: Goebbels.

*The Weakest Link*

ANNE ROBINSON: In Italian history, in 1919 which former journalist set up the Fascist party?

CONTESTANT: Silvio Berlusconi.

*The Weakest Link*

ANNE ROBINSON: The first Christmas radio broadcast given by George V in 1932 was scripted by which English poet and author?

CONTESTANT: Oliver Cromwell.

*The Weakest Link*

EAMONN HOLMES: What title did Edward VIII take after his abdication?

CONTESTANT: Edward the Confessor.

*Sudo-Q, BBC2*

MELANIE SYKES: What was the nickname given to Field Marshal Montgomery during the Second World War?

CONTESTANT: Lord Haw-Haw.

*The Vault*

ANNE ROBINSON: Which allied leader met with Stalin and Roosevelt at Yalta in February 1945?

CONTESTANT: Hitler.

*The Weakest Link*

ANNE ROBINSON: Who became US President after the death of Franklin Roosevelt in 1945?

CONTESTANT: Abraham Lincoln.

*The Weakest Link*

JOHN HUMPHRYS: What was the name of the peer who disappeared in 1974 after allegedly murdering his children's nanny, having mistaken her for his wife?

CONTESTANT: Lord Snowdon.

*Mastermind*

# MODERN LANGUAGES

ANNE ROBINSON: Which European language do the words blitz, kindergarten and angst come from?

CONTESTANT: Italian.

*The Weakest Link*

ANNE ROBINSON: The word 'croissant' literally means what shape?

CONTESTANT: Triangle.

*The Weakest Link*


ANNE ROBINSON: Cantonese and Mandarin are two languages that originated in which oriental country?

CONTESTANT: Spain.

*The Weakest Link*


ANNE ROBINSON: What is the official language of Israel?

CONTESTANT: Latin.

*The Weakest Link*

# MUSIC

STEVE WRIGHT: Who wrote the music for Moon River and also The Pink Panther?
CONTESTANT: Mendelssohn.

*Radio 2*


PHIL WOOD: Which famous classical composer went deaf?
CONTESTANT: Errr...
FEMALE CO-PRESENTER: Think of a big dog.
CONTESTANT: Bach.

*BBC GMR*


KEN BRUCE: Listen to this piece of music [Sex Crime by Eurythmics] and tell me the name of the movie it featured in, made from a famous George Orwell novel.
CONTESTANT: Was it 1989, Ken?

*Radio 2*


LES DENNIS: Name a part of the body mentioned in many love songs.
CONTESTANT: Clothes.

*Family Fortunes, Challenge*

EAMONN HOLMES: Dizzy Gillespie is
   famous for playing... what?
CONTESTANT: (after thinking a few seconds)
   Basketball.

*National Lottery Jet Set*

ANNE ROBINSON: According to the popular
   singer Katie Melua in one of her recent
   songs, there are how many bicycles in
   Beijing?
CONTESTANT: Ten?
ANNE ROBINSON: Nine million.

*The Weakest Link*

# DUMB WORLD

Presenter: Which 'pie' did both Don McLean and Madonna sing about?

Stroppy South African contestant: Don't know.

Presenter: Take a guess.

Contestant: Chicken pie.

Presenter: No. Come on, you know this. What type of 'pie' did both Don McLean and Madonna sing about?

Contestant: Cottage pie.

Presenter: No, it's a country. Last go. What type of 'pie' did both Don McLean and Madonna sing about? Famous song.

Contestant: (long pause) U.K. pie.

*Radio 2, Dubai,*
*UNITED ARAB EMIRATES*

RICHARD ALLINSON: Bob & Earl and the Rolling Stones had big hits singing about the Harlem... what?

CONTESTANT: Globetrotters.

*Radio 2*

ANDY TOWNSEND: The Beatles were known as the Fab...?

CALLER: Five.

*talkSPORT*

ANNE ROBINSON: Which piece of music by Tchaikovsky features explosions, cannon fire and gunshots?

CONTESTANT: The Flight of the Bumblebee.

*The Weakest Link*

ANNE ROBINSON: In music, which famous composer wrote a set of pieces known as 'the Enigma Variations'?

CONTESTANT: Andrew Lloyd Webber.

*The Weakest Link*

MELANIE SYKES: In which European city was the first opera house opened in 1637?

CONTESTANT: Sydney

*The Vault, ITV*

GARY KING: Which singing diva had a
    UK number one hit in the 1960s called
    'Respect'?

CONTESTANT: George Galloway?

*LBC 97.3*


QUESTIONMASTER: Who sang the song 'Je
    T'Aime' with Jane Birkin?

TWO CONTESTANTS (given a choice of three
    answers): Jacques Chirac.

*24 Hour Quiz, ITV*

# MYTH & LEGEND

CHRIS EVANS: Name ten mythical creatures in sixty seconds.

CONTESTANT: A tiger.

CHRIS EVANS: That's not mythical!

CONTESTANT: Erm, er, erm...

CHRIS EVANS: Think Lord Of The Rings...

CONTESTANT: Midgets and dwarves.

CHRIS EVANS: Midgets and dwarves are real!

CONTESTANT: (laughing) No they're not!

*Radio 2*

DAVE SPIKEY: What was the last thing left in Pandora's box?

CONTESTANT: (long pause) A brush?

*Bullseye, Challenge*

# POLITICS

ANNE ROBINSON: In the late 1970s the so-called 'Lib-Lab pact' was between Labour and which other political party?

CONTESTANT: The Conservatives.

*The Weakest Link*

NICK RISBY: Name Britain's first and only Jewish Prime Minister.

CONTESTANT: (after long deliberation) Is it Ariel Sharon?

*BBC Radio Suffolk*

RICHARD ALLINSON: Name the eccentric politician who has resigned as editor of The Spectator to concentrate on his political career with the Conservatives.

CONTESTANT: Boris Yeltsin.

*Radio 2*

ANNE ROBINSON: In Liverpool the Pie
And Gannex pub was named after which
Labour Prime Minister?

CONTESTANT: John Major.

*The Weakest Link*


MICHAEL BARRYMORE: Who was Prime
Minister when Britain joined the European
Community in 1973?

CONTESTANT: Neville Chamberlain.

*Strike It Rich, Challenge*


ANNE ROBINSON: In UK politics, which
party leader's surname is an anagram of
'romance'?

CHANTELLE from Big Brother: Love.

ROBINSON: No, it was David Cameron.

CHANTELLE from Big Brother: Who?

*The Weakest Link*


ANNE ROBINSON: MPs wanting to clear the
House of Commons public gallery used to
shout 'I spy...' what?

CONTESTANT: With my little eye.

*The Weakest Link*

ANNE ROBINSON: What was the abbreviation used for the branch of the civil service called Military Intelligence, section 6?

CONTESTANT: MI5.

*The Weakest Link*

ANNE ROBINSON: In government organisations, what does the letter M stand for in MI5 and MI6?

CONTESTANT: Murder.

*The Weakest Link*

PRESENTER: Which famous former foreign leader addressed the Labour Party Conference?

CONTESTANT: Gorbachev.

PRESENTER: No it was an American.

CONTESTANT: Lenin.

*BBC Southern Counties Radio*

COLIN MURRAY: This weekend marks the anniversary of the death of which notorious Russian dictator?

CONTESTANT: Erm... Hitler?

*Radio 1*

ANNE ROBINSON: What is the full name of Karl Marx's book: Das...?

CONTESTANT: Kampf.

*The Weakest Link*

ANNE ROBINSON: In London's congestion charge, which country's diplomats have collected the most penalties?

CONTESTANT: Wales.

*The Weakest Link*

JOHN HUMPHRYS: What two letters do members of the Welsh Assembly have after their names?

CONTESTANT: SS.

*Mastermind*

ANNE ROBINSON: Name the man who was president of Italy until May 2006.

CONTESTANT: Don Corleone.

*The Weakest Link*

ANNE ROBINSON: Juan Peron was twice President of which South American country?

CONTESTANT: Poland.

*The Weakest Link*

ANNE ROBINSON: In politics, what is the current occupation of David Blunkett?

CONTESTANT: Blind.

*The Weakest Link*

ANNE ROBINSON: Which single-issue political party was formed by Sir James Goldsmith in 1995 to campaign against European integration?

CONTESTANT: The Conservatives.

*The Weakest Link*

ANNE ROBINSON: Which British Prime Minister famously said, 'We have become a grandmother'?

CONTESTANT: John Major.

*The Weakest Link*

CARLOS: What former premier makes over £4 million a year as an after-dinner speaker?

CONTESTANT: David Beckham.

CARLOS: No, I'm looking for a former premier. Prime Minister or President...

CONTESTANT: Oh, Tony Blair.

CARLOS: No, think of someone smooth...

CONTESTANT: John Major?

CARLOS: No...

CONTESTANT: John Prescott.

CARLOS: No, I don't think he's ever been Prime Minister or President...

CONTESTANT: Oh, give us a clue, Carlos!

CARLOS: I'm trying, I'm trying. (pause) Look, just say 'Bill Clinton'.

CONTESTANT: Who?

*Wave 105*

# RELIGIOUS EDUCATION

ROY WALLER: On what day did God create Earth?

CONTESTANT: Was it a Tuesday?

*BBC Radio Norfolk*

ALAN BRAZIL: What was the name of the first man on Earth?

CONTESTANT: Tony.

*talkSPORT*

ANNE ROBINSON: According to the authorised version of the Bible, who was the first woman on Earth?

CONTESTANT: (after long pause) Mary.

*The Weakest Link*

ANNE ROBINSON: Which 'J' is a major figure in the New Testament whose mother is often called the Blessed Virgin Mary?

CONTESTANT: Pass.

*The Weakest Link*

ANNE ROBINSON: The name of which religious festival is sometimes shortened to 'Chrimbo'?

CONTESTANT: Ramadan.

*The Weakest Link*

JK OR JOEL: Name a berry associated with Christmas.

CONTESTANT: Ivory.

*Radio 1*

ANNE ROBINSON: Which city in Staffordshire beginning with 'L' has a cathedral with three spires?

CONTESTANT: Oswestry.

*The Weakest Link*

PRESENTER: Which Derbyshire town is famous for a church with a crooked spire?

CONTESTANT: Lincoln Cathedral.

*BBC Radio Bristol*

CALLER: It's a famous monument in Salisbury.

RICHARD MADELEY: Winchester Cathedral?

*'You Say We Pay', Richard And Judy, C4*

ANNE ROBINSON: The spiritual leader of Tibet is known by what two-word name?

CONTESTANT: The Rabbi.

*The Weakest Link*

WILLIAM G STEWART: Above the entrance to which place do the words 'Abandon all hope, ye who enter here' appear?

CONTESTANT: A church?

STEWART: Er sorry, no, hell.

*Fifteen-to-One, C4*

ANNE ROBINSON: In the traditional version of the Lord's Prayer, what 'H', meaning sanctified, goes before 'be they name'?

CONTESTANT (quietly): Howard.

ROBINSON (incredulously): Pardon?

CONTESTANT (louder): Howard.

*The Weakest Link*

WILLIAM G STEWART: Judaism. Who in the UK is the Chief Rabbi?

CONTESTANT: Lionel Blair.

*Fifteen-to-One*

PETER SNOW: What language was the Koran originally written in?

CONTESTANT: Er, Hebrew?

*Masterteam, Radio 4*

# SCIENCE & TECHNOLOGY

SARA COX: What does a meteorologist study?

CONTESTANT: Er, meteors?

*Radio 1*

DANNY KELLY: In which year did man first land on the moon?

CONTESTANT: Can I have a clue?

KELLY: OK. I was born in 1970. My brother is a year older and this was the year he was born in.

CONTESTANT: 1971.

*Radio WM*

ANNE ROBINSON: Which force keeps the moon in orbit around the earth, and the earth in orbit around the sun?

CONTESTANT (winner of the show): Delta Force.

*The Weakest Link*

ANNE ROBINSON: The seven stars in the formation referred to as 'the Plough' are part of the constellation called 'the Great...' what?

CONTESTANT: Gatsby.

*The Weakest Link*

## DUMB WORLD

PRESENTER: Beginning with K, what was the first name of the German car maker whose last name was Benz?

CONTESTANT: Bruce.

*Temptation, Channel 9, AUSTRALIA*

MATTHEW CARR: What was the destination of the Mariner 9 space probe?

CALLER: Plymouth.

*BBC Radio Shropshire*

STEVE WRIGHT: On this day in 1963, how did Valentina Tereshkova become famous?

CONTESTANT: Was she the first woman to grow a potato?

*Radio 2*

EAMONN HOLMES: What travels at 300 million metres a second?

CONTESTANT: A cheetah.

*Sudo-Q*

ANNE ROBINSON: Venus, Mars and Jupiter are all planets orbiting which celestial body?

CONTESTANT: (pauses to think) ...Earth?

*The Weakest Link*

STEVE WRIGHT: In which direction does the sun set?

CONTESTANT: North.

*Radio 2*

DALE WINTON: Which planet in our solar system is known as the 'red planet'. Mars, Jupiter or Mercury?

CONTESTANT: Well, I would say Jupiter, but that's the one with the rings around it.

*The National Lottery: In It To Win It*


COLIN (or possibly Edith): What 'A' is a compound, containing hydrogen, carbon and oxygen, that is produced when yeast makes sugar ferment?

CONTESTANT: Er, is it aluminium?

*Colin & Edith Show, Radio 1*


ALEX LOVELL: It has atomic number 13 and the abbreviation 'Al' and is silvery in colour. Which chemical element?

CONTESTANT: Gold.

*BrainTeaser, Five*


JEFF OWEN: Who invented the telescope and the thermometer?

CONTESTANT (long pause): Er...

JEFF OWEN: Think of 'Bohemian Rhapsody' and you'll get it.

CONTESTANT: Beelzebub?

*BBC Radio Nottingham*

GRAHAM LIVER: Which piece of essential household equipment was invented by Thomas Crapper?

CONTESTANT: Er...

LIVER: The clue's in the question. Thomas Crapper.

CONTESTANT: The tin opener?

*BBC Radio Leeds*

SADIE NINE: Which chemical element has the symbol K?

CONTESTANT: Kryptonite.

*BBC Radio London*

## DUMB WORLD

MARK FORSYTH: This year, the Ford Motor Company celebrated fifty years of production of one of its makes of cars by discontinuing the line. What was the make of car?

CONTESTANT: Was it the Tin Lizzie?

FORSYTH: No, much later. Fifty years ago: 1955.

CONTESTANT: Er, did you say the Ford Motor Company?

FORSYTH: That's right.

CONTESTANT: Er...

FORSYTH: Think of the Beach Boys, having fun, fun, fun, 'til her daddy takes the.... away.

CONTESTANT: Is it the Pinto?

*Almanac, CBC, CANADA*

ANNE ROBINSON: What is the round implement believed to have been invented around 4,000 years ago and used in transport ever since?

CONTESTANT: The steam engine.

*The Weakest Link*

ANDY TOWNSEND: How many wheels does a tricycle have?

CALLER: Two.

*Weekend Sports Breakfast, talkSPORT*

PRESENTER: It's a vessel with two hulls, connected by a frame. It can go very fast; what's its name?

CONTESTANT: A motorbike.

*Rhyming quiz, Radio 2*

STEVE WRIGHT: Which brothers made the first powered flight in North Carolina in 1903?

CONTESTANT: Erm, the Boeings?

*Radio 2*

STEVE WRIGHT: Where would you find a plimsoll line?

CONTESTANT: In a shoe.

*Radio 2*

# MULTIPLE CHOICE

ANNE ROBINSON: In the Middle Ages, Richard Neville, Earl of Warwick, was known as what, the Kingmaker or the Cakemaker?

CONTESTANT: The Cakemaker.

*The Weakest Link*

ANNE ROBINSON: What animal is stamped on eggs to show they have reached European standards, a lion or a chicken?

CONTESTANT: A chicken.

*The Weakest Link*

ANNE ROBINSON: Before he became Holy Roman Emperor, Charlemagne was king of whom, the Franks or the Brunos?

CONTESTANT: The Brunos.

*The Weakest Link*

ANNE ROBINSON: In Germany, the Burgermeister runs what: the local town hall or the local fast food outlet?

CONTESTANT: The local fast food outlet.

*The Weakest Link*

PRESENTER: What brand of luggage can also be found on the head of a deer, Samsonite or Antler?

CONTESTANT: Samsonite.

*Radio Broadland, Norfolk*

ANNE ROBINSON: Oscar Wilde, Adolf Hitler and Jeffrey Archer have all written books about their experiences in what: prison, or the Conservative Party?

CONTESTANT: The Conservative Party.

*The Weakest Link*

ANNE ROBINSON: "It's what your right arm's for" was a slogan advertising what type of product: beer or toilet paper?

CONTESTANT: Er, toilet paper.

*The Weakest Link*

ANNE ROBINSON: What is the religion of Japan: shinto or brillo?

CONTESTANT: Brillo.

*The Weakest Link*

## NOT SO DUMB AFTER ALL?

ANNE ROBINSON: The title of a well-known novel by Jeffrey Archer was 'First Among...' what?

CONTESTANT: Thieves.

*The Weakest Link*